BUILDINGS

Alessandro Vignozzi

Illustrated by
Giuseppe Arrighi, Giovanni Bernardi,
Simone Boni, Lorenzo Cecchi, L.R. Galante, Lorenzo Pieri,
Ivan Stalio, Stefano Tartarotti

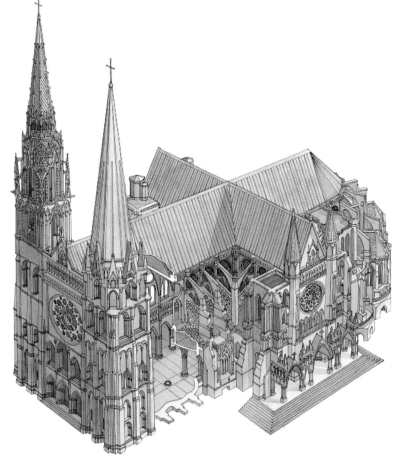

BARNES
&NOBLE
B O O K S
NEW YORK

DoGi

A Donati Giudici
Associati, Florence,
production.
Original title *Le
misure del tempo*
Text:
Caterina Rochat
Illustrations:
Alessandro
Bartolozzi,
Giovanni Bernardi,
Sergio
Designers:
Roberto Lari
Sabina Carandini

© 1995 By Donati
Giudici Associati srl
Florence,
Italy

First English edition
© 1995 Watts Books

First American edition
© 1997
Barnes & Noble, Inc.
This edition published
by Barnes & Noble, Inc.
by arrangement with
DoGi srl

ISBN
0-7607-0594-1

Printed in Italy

10 9 8 7 6 5 4 3 2 1

English translation by
Patricia Borlenghi

Edited by
Janet De Saulles

HOW TO USE THIS BOOK

SUBJECT
The introductory
paragraphs present
the main ideas in
each chapter.

EXPLANATION
The main subject is
brought to life with
beautiful large
illustrations. Short
captions draw
attention to
interesting details.

GLOSSARY
Technical or more
difficult words are
explained in the
glossary, found at
the back of the
book.

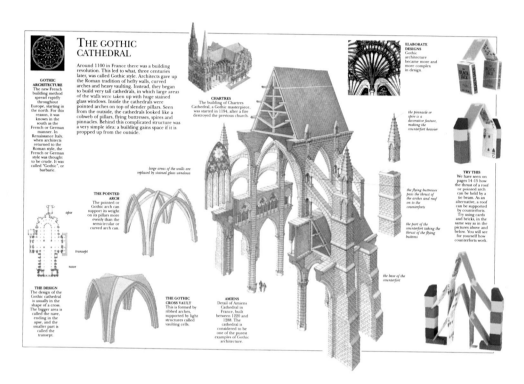

**HISTORICAL
BACKGROUND**
The historical
background of
each area is given,
and later
developments are
explored.

LEADING FIGURES
People who have
contributed to the
development of
different
inventions or
theories are
included.

EXPERIMENTS
Easy and enjoyable
experiments are
suggested, letting
the readers
discover for
themselves some
of the scientific
principles explored
in this book.

CREDITS

The illustrations in this book,
original and previously
unpublished, have been
produced under the direction of
DoGi srl, who holds copyright.
ILLUSTRATIONS: Giuseppe Arrighi
(12, 13, 14, 15, 22, 23); Giovanni
Bernardi (6, 7); Simone Boni (20,
21, 28, 29); Lorenzo Cecchi (18, 19,
26, 27, 30, 31, 40, 41); L.R. Galante
(8, 9, 42, 43); Lorenzo Pieri (16, 17,
34, 35); Ivan Stalio (4, 5, 10, 11, 12,
13, 24, 25, 32, 33, 36, 37, 38, 39);
Stefano Tartarotti (13, 14, 30a).
COVER: Giovanni Bernardi
PHOTOGRAPHS: DoGi's archives (5a,
7a, 10, 12, 17, 18, 25, 37, 43a, 43b);
Author's archives (5b, 20, 26b, 31,
32, 36, 39, 41b, 42a, 42b, 42c, 43c);
Carlo Cantini, Florence (5c, 14a,
14b, 14c, 16a, 16b, 40, 41a, 23a,
23b, 23c, 28b); Casabella archives

(7b, 7c); Foto Quilici (9); Réunion
des Musées Nationaux, Paris (26a);
Lewis W. Hine (28a).

DoGi srl has made every effort to
contact all the relevant copyright
holders and apologize for any
omissions or errors that may
have inadvertently been made.
Any eventual corrections will be
made in the next editions of this
work.

CONTENTS

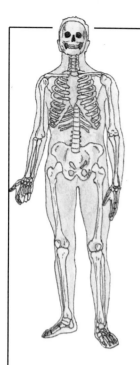

WHAT YOU WILL LEARN FROM THIS BOOK

In any building, new or old, some parts can be taken out without putting the building at risk. These include: certain partitions used inside the building, roof coverings, doors, windows and decorative features. Other parts of a building, however, are absolutely essential: without them, the building would not stand up. Such parts include supporting walls and load-bearing parts: beams, arches and vaults. Together, these parts make up the building's structure. There are no buildings without structure, even if the structure is invisible from the outside.

Not all structures, though, are the same. They can change, depending on the materials used. A wooden structure works differently from a steel one. Over the centuries, the design of structures has become more and more scientific. In ancient times, builders relied on common sense and experience. From the 17th century onwards, scientists worked on a theory of structures, which gradually allowed buildings to be planned with greater and greater accuracy.

THE BODY'S SKELETON
The body's skeleton and muscles form the structure of the human body, but are invisible from the outside. In the same way, building structures are often hidden by their coverings, making it hard for us to see just how fundamental they are.

HIDDEN STRUCTURES
The structures of many skyscrapers are covered by simple glass surfaces, hiding the complicated cage of pillars and beams which keep the buildings standing.

ANIMALS AND HUMANS
Animals such as birds, squirrels, and monkeys are born with a sense of structure, automatically understanding the strong or weak parts of trees. They rarely break the branches they sit on. Humans do not have this natural gift. To work out how to make things balance, and to keep them stable, they have developed an area of science known as statics.

STRUCTURES THAT YOU CAN SEE
Bridges, Gothic cathedrals and various other buildings, such as the Eiffel Tower, show their structures. Part of the beauty of these buildings is due to the fact that they show off how they are built.

4

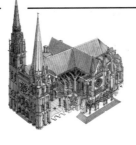

CAREFUL BUILDERS

Many ancient buildings, such as the Colosseum, seem as beautiful today as they did when they were first built. This is thanks to the skill of the builders and, particularly, to their care. Where they were not sure of the exact measurements needed to make the building stable, to be on the safe side, they made walls, pillars and vaults as big as possible.

CARELESS BUILDERS

Gothic cathedrals are surprisingly light in structure. Medieval builders made use of very thin walls, and the buildings were actually supported on slender pillars. The builders did not have a science of building, but trusted in their own judgment. While some cathedrals lasted, many others collapsed.

HOW SCIENTISTS HELPED BUILDERS

From the 17th century on, the study of structural problems passed from architects to scientists. A theory was devised which slowly allowed structures to be planned in exact detail. The modern engineer is both a technician and a mathematician.

WHAT IS STATICS?

Statics is the area of physics where the balance of solid bodies, including the balance of buildings, is studied. Buildings have to be able to support their own weight, and the weight of the things in them. They also have to be able to resist powerful winds and earthquakes.

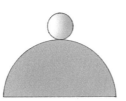

INSTABILITY

The table-tennis ball in the above picture is unsteady. If hit, it will roll to the bottom.

STABILITY

The table tennis ball is now steady. It can react to any hit, always finding its original position.

MAKING BUILDINGS STABLE

Building a house of cards is a game of balance. It will stand if the cards are placed very carefully on each other. This balance can easily be upset, however, as a breath is enough to knock it over. A building is also the result of a game of balance. It has to be stable and secure so that nothing can make it fall down.

ENGINEERS AND ARCHITECTS

Once architects were also engineers. As well as drawing up building plans, they had to find solutions to technical problems. From the 18th century on, the professions divided. Engineers began to specialize in structural planning, while architects concentrated on the designs for the shape and layout of buildings.

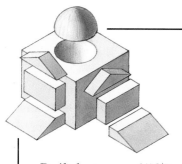

THE PARTS OF A BUILDING

The Italian Villa Almerico, known as the Rotonda, is one of the most admired buildings in the world. Built between 1567 and 1569 by the Venetian architect Palladio, it was soon seen as a masterpiece which had no equal. Illustrations of the villa, drawn by Palladio in his *Four Books on Architecture,* quickly became world famous: over three centuries of architects studied and copied them. Buildings inspired by the Rotonda are found in England, France, Spain, Russia and the United States. This Italian Renaissance building is a magnificent example of the technical knowledge found behind the beauty of classical architecture. From its foundations through to its roof, it shows the main features of classical architecture.

ANDREA PALLADIO
(1508-80)
One of the major Italian Renaissance architects, he was born of humble origins in Vicenza. He became favorite architect to the most powerful Venetian families, building their villas and palaces. Palladio often visited Rome to study its ancient monuments.

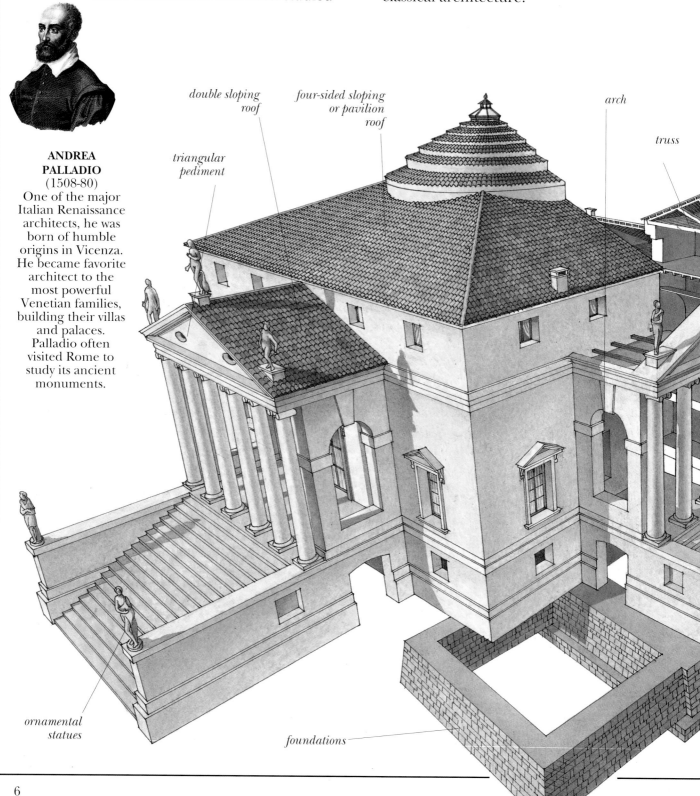

double sloping roof

four-sided sloping or pavilion roof

arch

truss

triangular pediment

ornamental statues

foundations

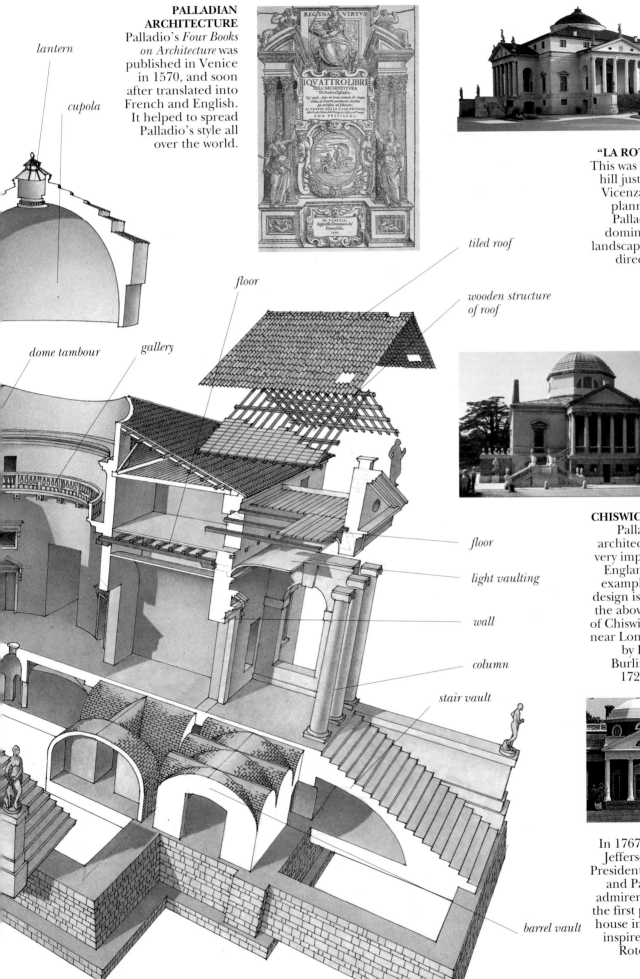

PALLADIAN ARCHITECTURE
Palladio's *Four Books on Architecture* was published in Venice in 1570, and soon after translated into French and English. It helped to spread Palladio's style all over the world.

lantern

cupola

dome tambour

gallery

floor

tiled roof

wooden structure of roof

"LA ROTONDA"
This was built on a hill just outside Vicenza. It was planned by Palladio to dominate the landscape in every direction.

floor

light vaulting

wall

column

stair vault

CHISWICK HOUSE
Palladian architecture was very important in England. One example of the design is shown in the above picture of Chiswick House, near London, built by Lord Burlington, 1720-25.

In 1767 Thomas Jefferson, U.S. President, architect and Palladian admirer, drew up the first plans for a house in Virginia, inspired by the Rotonda.

barrel vault

WHY DO BUILDINGS NEED FOUNDATIONS?

Have you ever noticed how difficult it is to walk on fresh snow? Skis were invented so that people could walk on snow without sinking or falling over. This is possible because the weight of our bodies normally concentrated on a small space – the sole – is spread over a wider area when we wear skis.

Foundations follow the same principle: the walls of buildings are not laid directly on the ground, but are built on a larger base to give stability. A house without foundations will not fall down immediately (the land on which buildings are erected is stronger than snow!), but it will cave in slowly. First, cracks will appear in the walls, and then the entire building might collapse. The cracks you see on the walls of old buildings are normally signs of bad foundations.

STABILITY
Every object is pushed down by its own weight. To keep it still an equal and opposite push is needed from the place where the object is resting.

ADDING UP
For centuries builders depended only on their own experience. Now the size of foundations is determined by the weight that a particular type of land can cope with. A little more than a square yd (a square m) of boggy land can only support one ton, while rocky soil can support up to 300 tons.

THE PLINTH
Modern reinforced-concrete buildings are placed on pillars instead of walls. These pillars are positioned on supports called plinths.

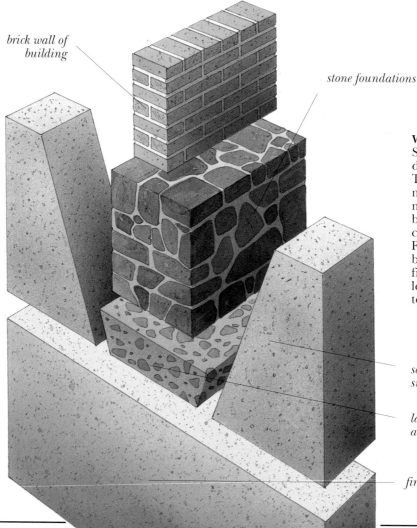

brick wall of building

stone foundations

WHY DIG?
Soil is made up of different layers. The top layer is made of organic material, and is brittle and crumbly. Foundations must be built on a firmer, stronger level, below this top layer.

soil with organic substances

layer of cement and stone

firm ground

FOUNDATIONS OF VENICE
The buildings of Venice are supported by long oak poles, planted into the firmest part of the lagoon floor.

SUBSIDENCE
Despite the long poles, Venetian buildings are not as stable as those on dry land. There are signs that the foundations of many buildings are slowly sinking or subsiding.

water

stone

firm part of lagoon floor

oak palings

THE WEIGHT OF THE PYRAMIDS
Cheop's Pyramid weighs 6,500,000 tons! But as this enormous mass is built on a base of more than 60,000 square yards (50,000 m^2), the average weight per square yard is "only" 130 tons, a load which the rocky soil can fully support.

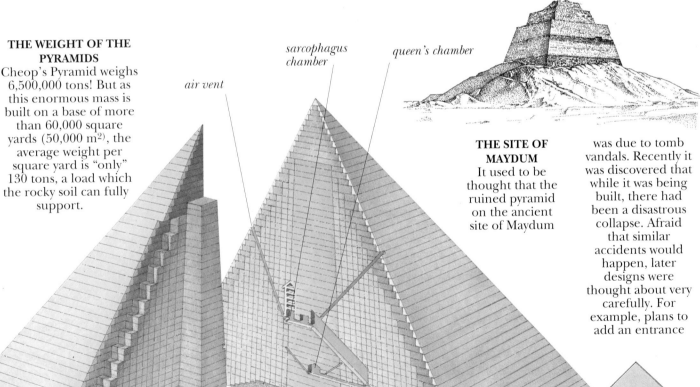

air vent

sarcophagus chamber

queen's chamber

THE SITE OF MAYDUM
It used to be thought that the ruined pyramid on the ancient site of Maydum was due to tomb vandals. Recently it was discovered that while it was being built, there had been a disastrous collapse. Afraid that similar accidents would happen, later designs were thought about very carefully. For example, plans to add an entrance on the side of one of Dahshur's pyramids were abandoned.

The pyramid's weight is heaviest at its center and at the lower parts of its sides, so builders inserted a stronger platform at the base of the center.

THE TOWER OF PISA

Soon after the Tower of Pisa was started, subsidence or sinking in the soil made the Tower lean dangerously. There had been a huge error in planning what size the foundations should be. Work was stopped but, after years of uncertainty and discussion, it was decided to finish the building and try to stop the tilt.

This was a risky decision. The safest thing would have been to knock the building down, and to rebuild it absolutely straight, on solid foundations. Who would have thought that in spite of leaning, the tower would remain standing? Centuries later scientists were able to see that a basic law of balance – the center of gravity or barycenter – was being followed.

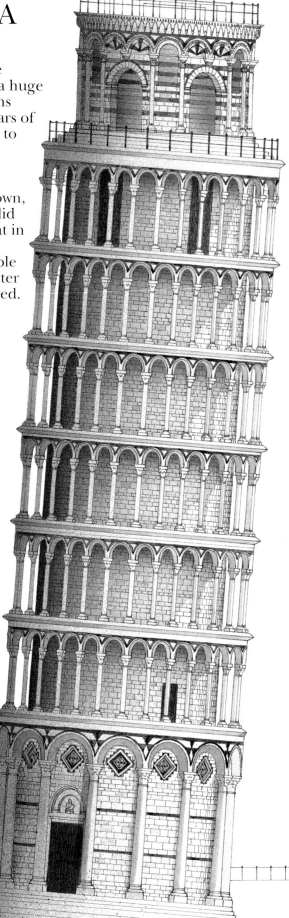

PLUMB LINE
The rule of thumb for every building is that the walls have to be perfectly straight. For centuries, builders used plumb lines made of lead to check this. Today, lasers are used to make sure that the walls of very tall buildings such as skyscrapers are straight.

THE TOWER OF PISA
Building work started in 1173. Shortly after, it began to tilt because of swampy soil and bad foundations. Despite its tilt, work continued and the Tower was completed in 1372. The Tower still leans today, although heavy lead blocks have recently been attached, helping to counterbalance the leaning.

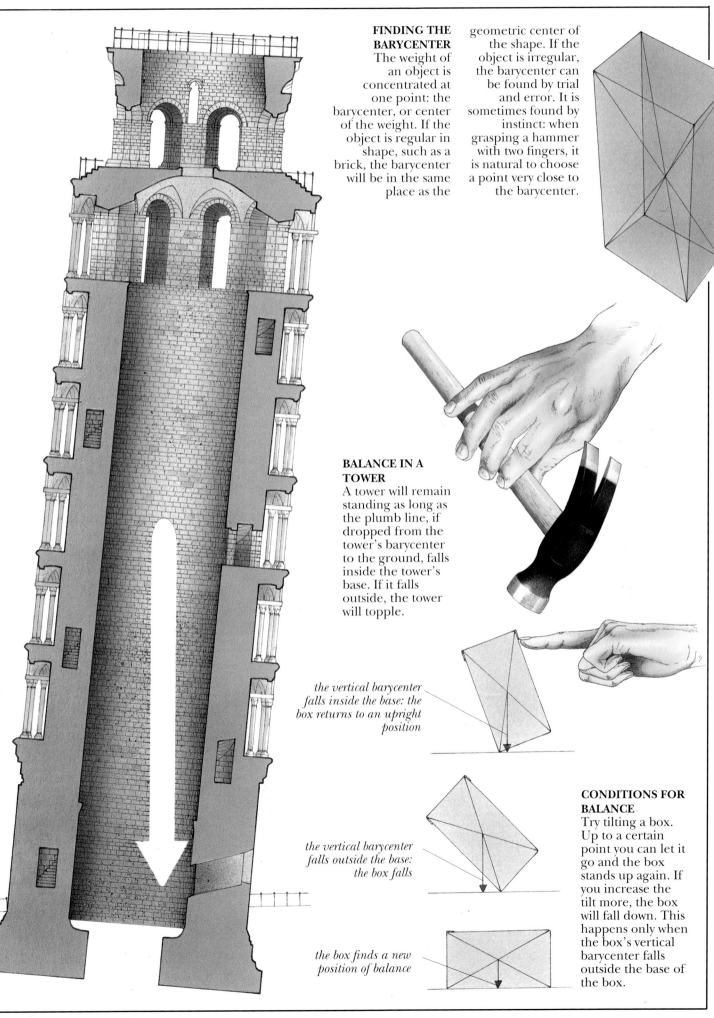

FINDING THE BARYCENTER

The weight of an object is concentrated at one point: the barycenter, or center of the weight. If the object is regular in shape, such as a brick, the barycenter will be in the same place as the geometric center of the shape. If the object is irregular, the barycenter can be found by trial and error. It is sometimes found by instinct: when grasping a hammer with two fingers, it is natural to choose a point very close to the barycenter.

BALANCE IN A TOWER

A tower will remain standing as long as the plumb line, if dropped from the tower's barycenter to the ground, falls inside the tower's base. If it falls outside, the tower will topple.

the vertical barycenter falls inside the base: the box returns to an upright position

the vertical barycenter falls outside the base: the box falls

the box finds a new position of balance

CONDITIONS FOR BALANCE

Try tilting a box. Up to a certain point you can let it go and the box stands up again. If you increase the tilt more, the box will fall down. This happens only when the box's vertical barycenter falls outside the base of the box.

11

VERTICAL AND HORIZONTAL

A building is made of upright parts such as walls, columns and pillars. These support the building's weight and, because of this, are called load-bearers. It is also made up of horizontal parts, or suspensions. These are the floors under our feet and the ceilings over our heads.

In some ancient buildings the same material, stone, was used for load-bearers and suspensions. Three stones, two vertical and one horizontal, were used. Egyptian and Greek temples were built using this method. However, although stone is excellent for walls, it is not so good for floors. As it is a rigid material, it shatters easily. In later centuries, floors were built with wood. This is a flexible material, and more resistant to stress than stone is.

FLOORS
Building a floor can be a problem. If it is only supported at its ends, and not in the center, it will bend and finally break.

THE TRILITH
A trilith is made up of two vertical stones, called piers or pillars, and a horizontal stone, called an architrave.
The stone circle at Stonehenge, England, built 4,000 years ago, is made solely of triliths. Today we use the terms "post" for pillar, and "lintel" for architrave.

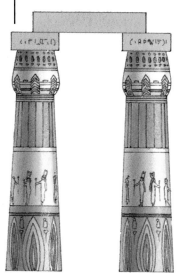

EGYPT
Egyptian temples were built by skillfully joining a series of triliths.

wooden planking

beams made as simple shafts

stone wall

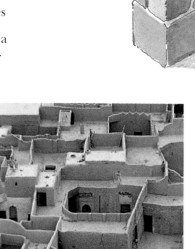

FLOOR OR ROOF?
In some countries with low rainfall, such as Morocco, roofs may also be used as floors (see left). The roofs are waterproofed by a thick layer of earth and lime.

TRY THIS
Place a sponge on two supports and press down on it. Its fibers get shorter on the side facing upwards because of compression. They get longer along the bottom because of traction. The same warping, even though it is usually far less noticeable, happens to every material which is resting on its ends – be it stone, wood or steel.

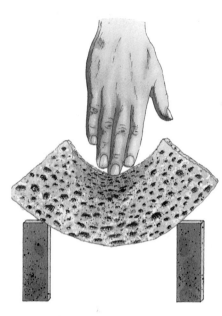

traction   *compression*

TRACTION AND COMPRESSION
The different parts of a building are built to resist these two types of stress. Floors are subject to traction and compression and can resist both. Walls, however, can only resist compression stress.

small parapet for collecting rainwater

waterproofing plaster

gutter for water flow

layer of earth, lime and sand

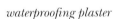

RIGID MATERIALS
Stone is a rigid material. It can cope well with compression, but copes badly with traction. Because of this, stone floors and architraves tend to break easily.

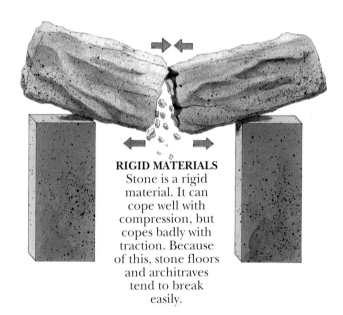

MORE STORIES
The wall and floor system allows buildings to have a number of stories.

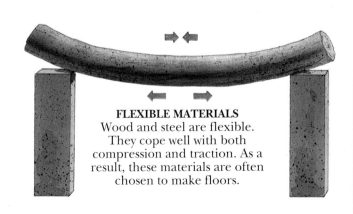

FLEXIBLE MATERIALS
Wood and steel are flexible. They cope well with both compression and traction. As a result, these materials are often chosen to make floors.

13

FROM HUT TO ROOF

The triangular-shaped hut was, perhaps, the first type of building to be invented. It is certainly the most simple building that exists. It offers good protection against the rain – it is not an accident that roofs in areas of high rainfall have the shape of a triangle. This type of building, however, has one main defect: the space inside it is very uncomfortable. So, a long time ago, somebody had the idea of raising the hut and setting it on two walls.

The first raised huts did not work well: the sloping roofs pressed down on the walls, making them fall over. The problem could be solved in two ways: the walls could either be propped up from the outside, or they could be joined together inside the hut. This second idea was the easiest and cheapest solution – and so the practice of using roof beams began.

EVOLUTION
The first simple huts were placed straight on the soil. By putting a hut on top of two walls, and joining it with a level beam, two advantages were found. The building, like the earlier triangular hut, offered protection against the rain. Secondly, this design provided extra space.

EXPERIMENT
1. Find three cards, some sticky tape and two empty playing card boxes.
2. Join two of the cards together with the tape, as in the above picture.

3. Use the empty boxes to make the walls of a model house. Put the two taped cards on top of the walls to make a roof. The pressure of the cards tends to push the walls over.

4. Now tape the third card to the base of the first two. Can you see how it stops the walls falling over?

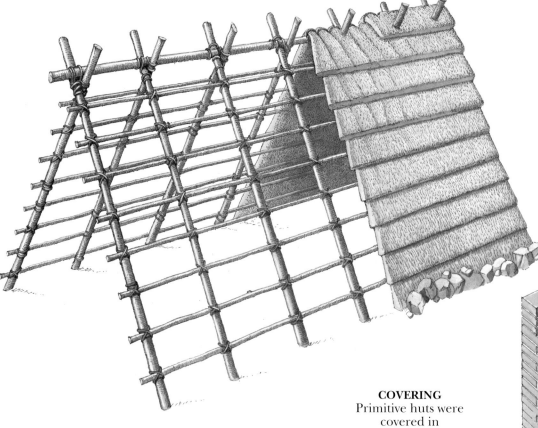

COVERING
Primitive huts were covered in overlapping layers of straw.

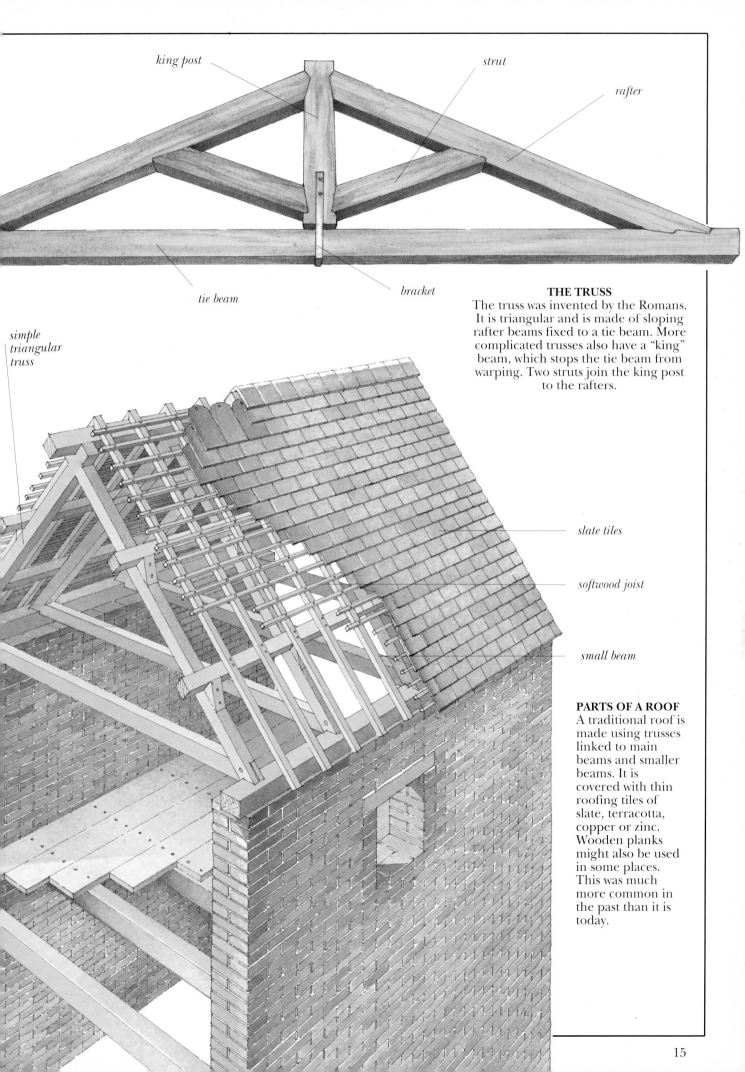

king post

strut

rafter

tie beam

bracket

THE TRUSS
The truss was invented by the Romans. It is triangular and is made of sloping rafter beams fixed to a tie beam. More complicated trusses also have a "king" beam, which stops the tie beam from warping. Two struts join the king post to the rafters.

simple triangular truss

slate tiles

softwood joist

small beam

PARTS OF A ROOF
A traditional roof is made using trusses linked to main beams and smaller beams. It is covered with thin roofing tiles of slate, terracotta, copper or zinc. Wooden planks might also be used in some places. This was much more common in the past than it is today.

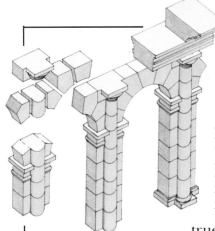

THE ARCH

It is often thought that the Romans invented the arch. In fact, the Babylonians and Egyptians had used it before them. What is true, is that the Romans were the first to see the potential of the arch, if used intelligently. By using it to replace wooden beams, building methods were completely changed. Wooden beams are limited by their length, which are not often longer than about 25 feet (eight meters) the height of the tallest trees used. Another problem with wood is that, over time, wood loses its strength, and decays. Using arches made of solid stone, the Romans could cover much greater spaces and build magnificent aqueducts or bridges. Some of these are still standing after 2,000 years.

THE WEAKNESS OF THE HORIZONTAL BEAM
A card placed on two boxes will bend if a weight is placed on it.

THE STRENGTH OF THE ARCH
By folding the same card into an arched shape, and holding it in position with two pins, the card can support a heavier weight. The arch shape gives the card much greater strength.

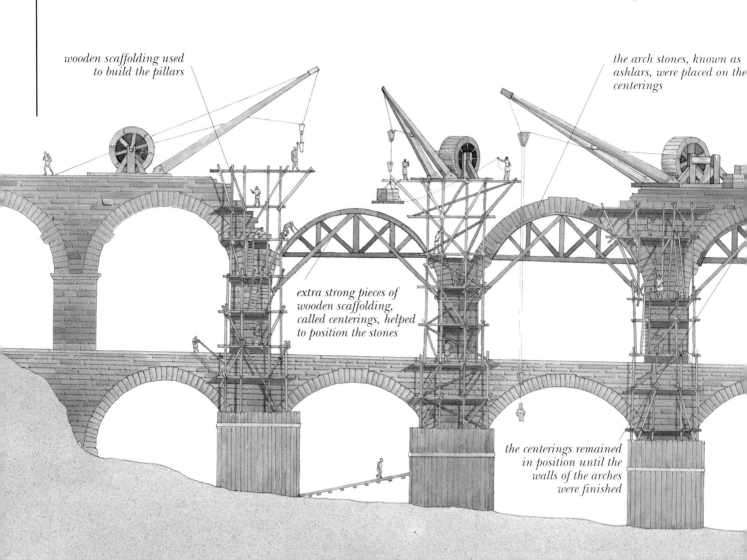

wooden scaffolding used to build the pillars

the arch stones, known as ashlars, were placed on the centerings

extra strong pieces of wooden scaffolding, called centerings, helped to position the stones

the centerings remained in position until the walls of the arches were finished

THRUST
The weight, or thrust, of the arch pushes down on its supports. In the 16th century, Leonardo da Vinci tried to calculate its weight by using counter weights.

THE TIE BEAM
In many buildings the thrust of an arch is held by an iron brace called a tie beam.

AQUEDUCT
Built around 19 BC, the Pont du Gard is one of the longest Roman aqueducts. It carries drinking water to the city of Nîmes in France from the surrounding hills. For most of the way (over 25 miles or 40 km) the aqueduct is buried. Bridges such as the Pont du Gard are used to cross valleys.

a system of small arches supports the canal

The Romans used cranes to lift the stones - men ran inside the wheels, making them turn, allowing the cranes to operate.

the centerings are dismantled

the largest arches of the aqueduct are those nearest the river

River Gard

FROM ARCH TO VAULT

A gallery is made by joining a number of arches, one behind the other. From this simple start Roman architects, inventing rows of vaults, or vaults and arches, were able to cover enormous spaces using only a few strong pillars. The humble mason, as well as the architect, must be given credit for this idea. Indeed, it was the Roman masons who invented cement, which allowed big blocks to be held together. This cement was made by mixing lime and a volcanic sand (from Pozzuoli, near Naples). As it set, the cement became hard, like stone.

THE COLOSSEUM
Built around AD 75 and known as the Colosseo, it is 620 ft (189 m) long and 157 ft (47 m) high and can seat 50,000 people. In spite of its enormous size, it was built in a short period of time, using the clever vaulting structure.

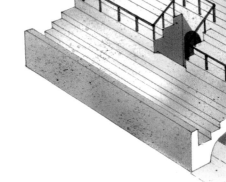

groin   *rib*

GROINS AND RIBS
If a stone cutter cuts a barrel vault diagonally, four pieces are formed: two groins and two ribs

BUILDING A VAULT
A vault is built in the same way as an arch (see page 16). The stone or cemented brick ashlars, placed on centerings, are removed at the end of the work.

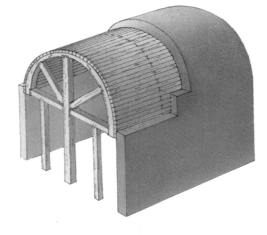

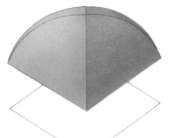

PAVILION VAULT
A pavilion arch is formed by joining four ribs together.

CROSS VAULT
A cross vault is formed by joining four groins together.

VAULTING
The tiers of
seats in the
Colosseum
were held up
by a
complicated
vaulting
system. Many
vaults are
built in a
circular
pattern.
Others are
built in rows,
for example
those which
give support
to the stairs.

DOMES

An overturned basket is a good example of a dome structure. A series of arches meet at the center, and hoops tied to them prevent the arches from opening. With modern materials, such as reinforced concrete, it is quite simple to build similar domes. In ancient times, however, the problem was much greater. Although the Romans knew how to build big, strong stone arches, such arches were very heavy. How could these be prevented from breaking under their own weight? Which materials or devices might be used to the same effect as basket circles? Here are some of the most famous attempts to find an answer.

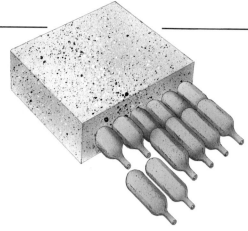

INTERLOCKING CONTAINERS
Byzantine builders used an ingenious system for making domes lighter: they used empty containers, one fitting inside the other.

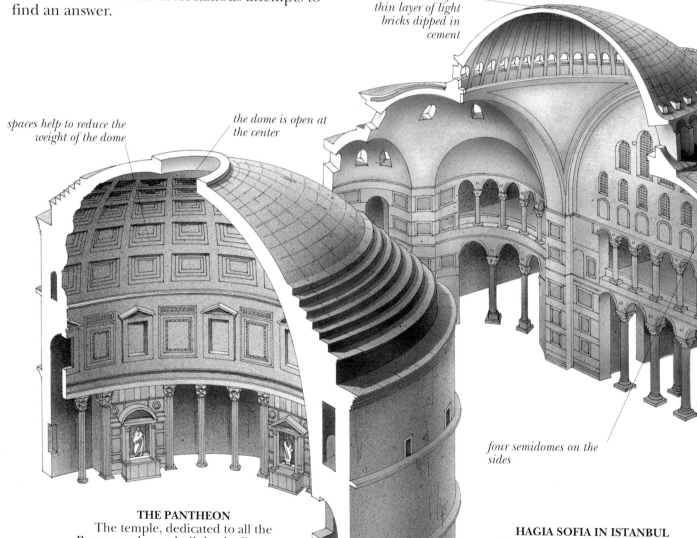

the dome is made of a thin layer of light bricks dipped in cement

spaces help to reduce the weight of the dome

the dome is open at the center

four semidomes on the sides

THE PANTHEON
The temple, dedicated to all the Roman gods, was built by the Emperor Hadrian in 124 BC. The 141 ft (43 m) diameter dome is made of Roman cement and lightened by empty spaces. The dome is supported by a wall 23 ft (7 m) thick.

HAGIA SOFIA IN ISTANBUL
The central dome of Hagia Sofia church is 105 ft (32 m) in diameter. It was built by the Emperor Justinian around AD 533. The dome is stable because it is thin and light, and because it is supported by four curved triangles, known as pendentives.

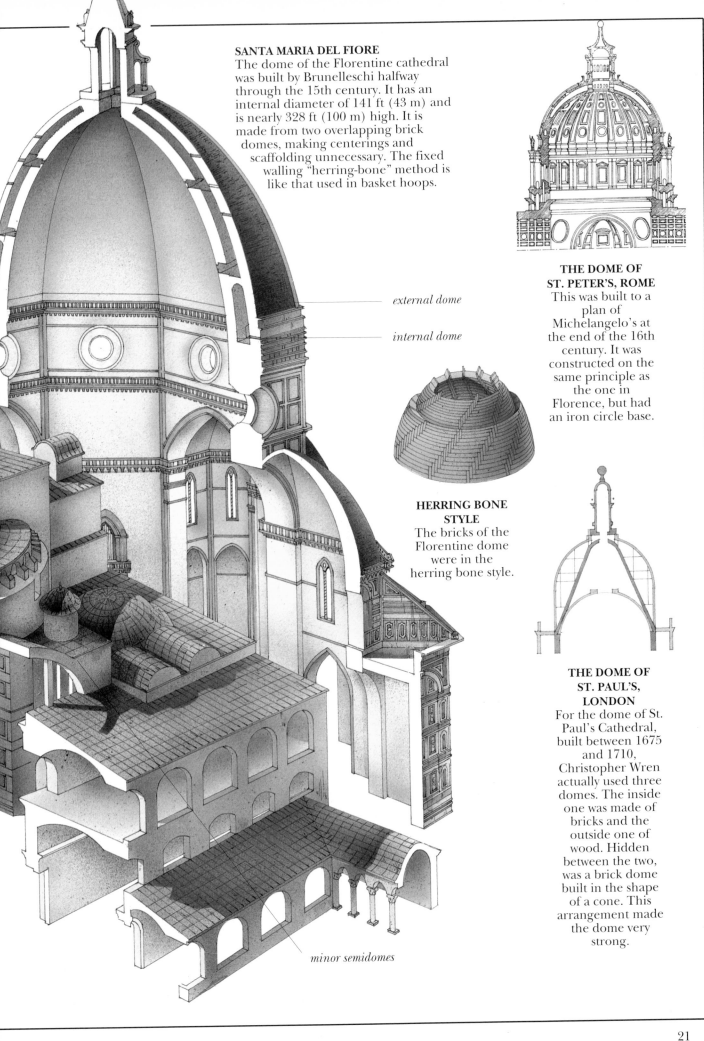

SANTA MARIA DEL FIORE
The dome of the Florentine cathedral was built by Brunelleschi halfway through the 15th century. It has an internal diameter of 141 ft (43 m) and is nearly 328 ft (100 m) high. It is made from two overlapping brick domes, making centerings and scaffolding unnecessary. The fixed walling "herring-bone" method is like that used in basket hoops.

external dome

internal dome

THE DOME OF ST. PETER'S, ROME
This was built to a plan of Michelangelo's at the end of the 16th century. It was constructed on the same principle as the one in Florence, but had an iron circle base.

HERRING BONE STYLE
The bricks of the Florentine dome were in the herring bone style.

THE DOME OF ST. PAUL'S, LONDON
For the dome of St. Paul's Cathedral, built between 1675 and 1710, Christopher Wren actually used three domes. The inside one was made of bricks and the outside one of wood. Hidden between the two, was a brick dome built in the shape of a cone. This arrangement made the dome very strong.

minor semidomes

THE GOTHIC CATHEDRAL

Around 1100 in France there was a building revolution. This led to what, three centuries later, was called Gothic style. Architects gave up the Roman tradition of hefty walls, curved arches and heavy vaulting. Instead, they began to build very tall cathedrals, in which large areas of the walls were taken up with huge stained glass windows. Inside the cathedrals were pointed arches on top of slender pillars. Seen from the outside, the cathedrals looked like a cobweb of pillars, flying buttresses, spires and pinnacles. Behind this complicated structure was a very simple idea: a building gains space if it is propped up from the outside.

GOTHIC ARCHITECTURE
The new French building method spread rapidly throughout Europe, starting in the north. For this reason, it was known in the south as the French or German manner. In Renaissance Italy, when architects returned to the Roman style, the French or German style was thought to be crude. It was called "Gothic", or barbaric.

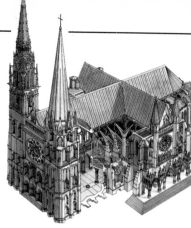

CHARTRES
The building of Chartres Cathedral, a Gothic masterpiece, was started in 1194, after a fire destroyed the previous church.

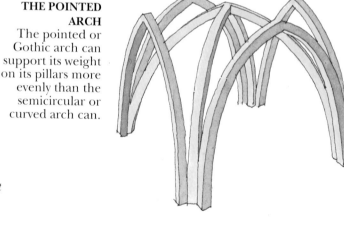

large areas of the walls are replaced by stained glass windows

THE POINTED ARCH
The pointed or Gothic arch can support its weight on its pillars more evenly than the semicircular or curved arch can.

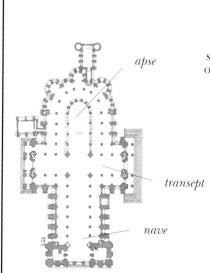

apse

transept

nave

THE DESIGN
The design of the Gothic cathedral is usually in the shape of a cross. The bigger area is called the nave, ending in the apse, and the smaller part is called the transept.

THE GOTHIC CROSS VAULT
This is formed by ribbed arches, supported by light structures called vaulting cells.

AMIENS
Detail of Amiens Cathedral in France, built between 1220 and 1288. The cathedral is considered to be one of the purest examples of Gothic architecture.

ELABORATE DESIGNS
Gothic architecture became more and more complex in design.

the pinnacle or spire is a decorative feature, making the counterfort heavier

the flying buttresses pass the thrust of the arches and roof on to the counterforts

the part of the counterfort taking the thrust of the flying buttress

the base of the counterfort

BLACK JACK

TRY THIS
We have seen on pages 14-15 how the thrust of a roof or pointed arch can be held by a tie beam. As an alternative, a roof can be supported by counterforts. Try using cards and bricks, in the same way as in the pictures above and below. You will see for yourself how counterforts work.

WOOD: A FORGOTTEN MATERIAL

OAK
Oak is one of the most-used building woods in central Europe. It is insect resistant and very strong.

In the past, when forests covered a large part of the planet, wood was the cheapest and most common material for house building. Stone was much more expensive and was mainly used for monuments, such as temples, churches, palaces and castles.

As well as being used for floors, roofs, doors and windows, wood was also used for the insides of buildings. This custom was continued for a long time in northern Europe, Turkey, Japan and China – in those mountainous areas where wood is plentiful. Wood-building techniques in North America developed quite spectacularly halfway through the 19th century, due to the invention of a system called the "balloon frame" (see opposite page).

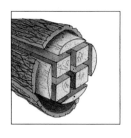

CUTTING METHODS
Some of the most common cutting methods.

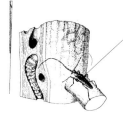

different types of wood borers

ENEMIES OF WOOD
Deathwatch beetles, woodworm and termites attack most kinds of woods. Woods most resistant to insects are: cypress, larch, oak, olive and ash.

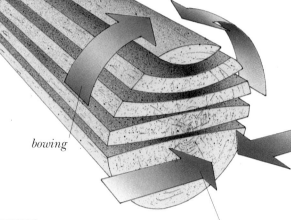

bowing

shrinking

WARPING
The main problem with wood is that it warps. As it dries, the trunk shrinks or bows.

FRAMEWORK
Traditional wooden French, German and English houses have structures made of beams and pillars, nailed to fixed joints. Walls might be made of earth, brick or braided rushes, coated in earth and lime.

FIR WOOD

The slender trunk of the fir tree provides long and straight pieces of wood. It is used in northern Europe and in mountainous areas. It can, however, be attacked by beetles such as wood borers.

OVERLAPPING TRUNKS

This technique is very old. Woods most commonly used are fir and larch, both of which stand up well in bad weather.

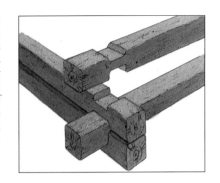

BALLOON FRAME

This building method is common all over the U.S. The insides of the buildings are constructed with a basic building plank called a two-by-four. The planks are placed, so that the buildings are particularly strong.

mortise

ASSEMBLY

In traditional wooden buildings, metal nails were not used. The various parts were joined by using the tenon – the protruding part of the fixed joint; the mortise – the hollow part of the fixed joint; and pegs – special wooden nails.

peg

tenon

POLISHED WOOD

Builders have recently started to use materials such as plywood. This is made from several thin planks glued together. Special varnishes protect the plywood from damp and woodworm.

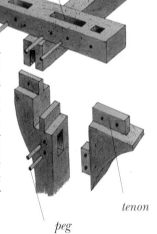

THE IRON AGE

Until quite recently, iron was both rare and expensive. It was used in the Middle Ages for making tools and knights' armor, rather than for building. With the Industrial Revolution, however, at the end of the 18th century, it was mined in great quantities and at better prices. Cast iron was made from a mixture of iron and carbon, and was able to support loads a hundred times greater than stone was able to.

ALEXANDRE GUSTAVE EIFFEL
(1832 - 1923)
Alexandre Gustave Eiffel, the French engineer, was one of the major forces behind the use of iron in building.

Engineers, before architects, soon realized the great possibilities that iron and cast iron gave builders, and the first daring light metal bridges were made. Around 1850, industrially produced steel replaced both cast iron and iron. The first step towards the skyscraper was taken.

GARABIT BRIDGE
The Garabit Bridge in France, built by Eiffel in 1870, is one of the most daring railroad bridges ever made.

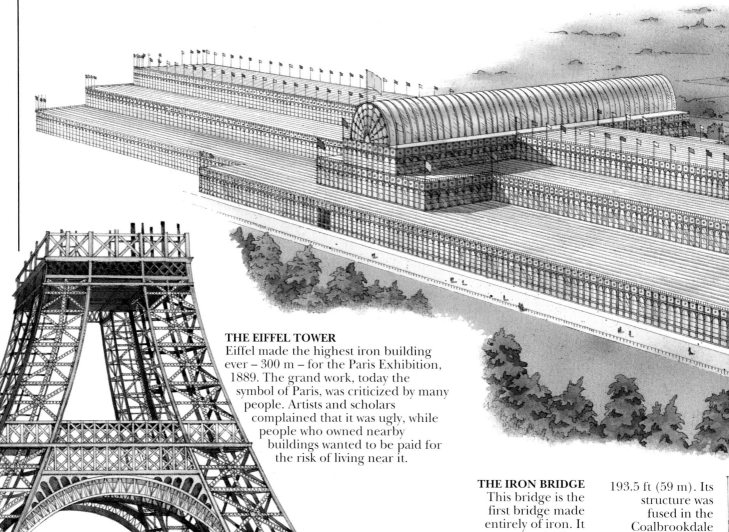

THE EIFFEL TOWER
Eiffel made the highest iron building ever – 300 m – for the Paris Exhibition, 1889. The grand work, today the symbol of Paris, was criticized by many people. Artists and scholars complained that it was ugly, while people who owned nearby buildings wanted to be paid for the risk of living near it.

THE IRON BRIDGE
This bridge is the first bridge made entirely of iron. It was built in England by Abraham Darby in 1779 and has a huge span of 193.5 ft (59 m). Its structure was fused in the Coalbrookdale steelworks nearby, famous for the part they played during the Industrial Revolution.

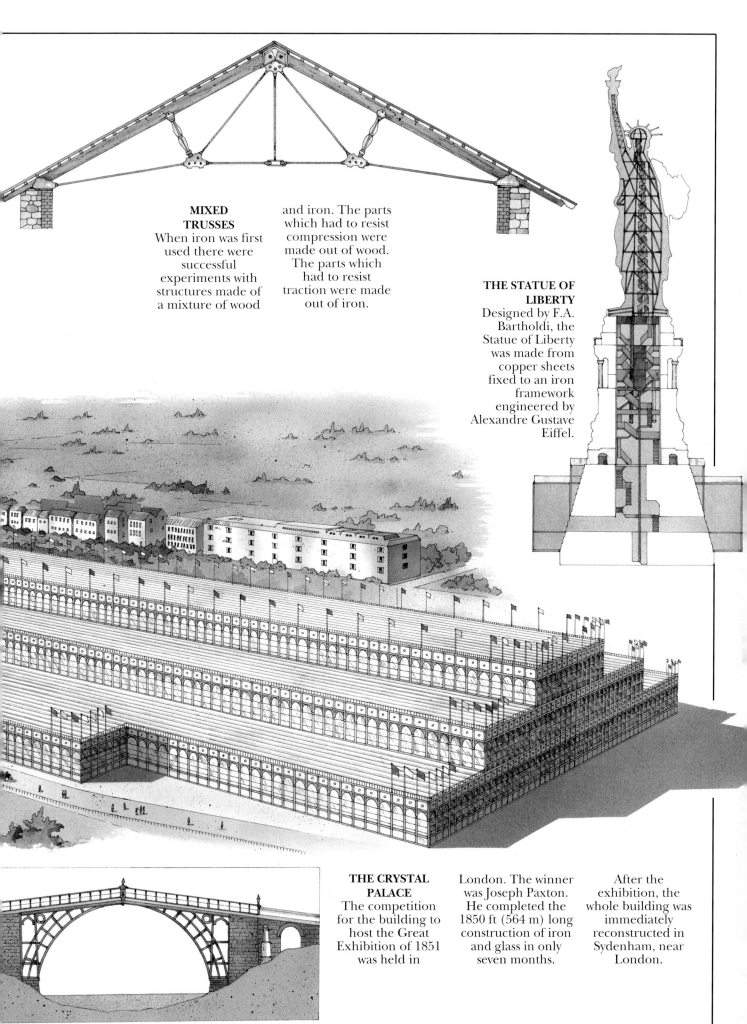

MIXED TRUSSES
When iron was first used there were successful experiments with structures made of a mixture of wood and iron. The parts which had to resist compression were made out of wood. The parts which had to resist traction were made out of iron.

THE STATUE OF LIBERTY
Designed by F.A. Bartholdi, the Statue of Liberty was made from copper sheets fixed to an iron framework engineered by Alexandre Gustave Eiffel.

THE CRYSTAL PALACE
The competition for the building to host the Great Exhibition of 1851 was held in London. The winner was Joseph Paxton. He completed the 1850 ft (564 m) long construction of iron and glass in only seven months. After the exhibition, the whole building was immediately reconstructed in Sydenham, near London.

THE SKYSCRAPER

At the end of the 19th century, the largest North American cities, such as New York and Chicago, saw the construction of many new buildings. They were so tall that it seemed natural to call them skyscrapers. There were three main reasons for this building explosion. The first was the lack of space in the cities – builders wanted to make the most of what room there was. The second was that steel allowed the design of very tall and light buildings. The third reason, which for a time seemed insignificant but in fact was decisive, was the invention of the elevator. Without this it would have been difficult to climb up to the hundredth floor!

STEEL STRUCTURE
The steel structure of the Empire State Building was completed by a team of 300 workers in only 23 weeks.

the outside walls are made of steel panels

THE ELEVATOR
The first elevators, such as the one shown above, were moved by hydraulic pumps. These were soon replaced by electric motors.

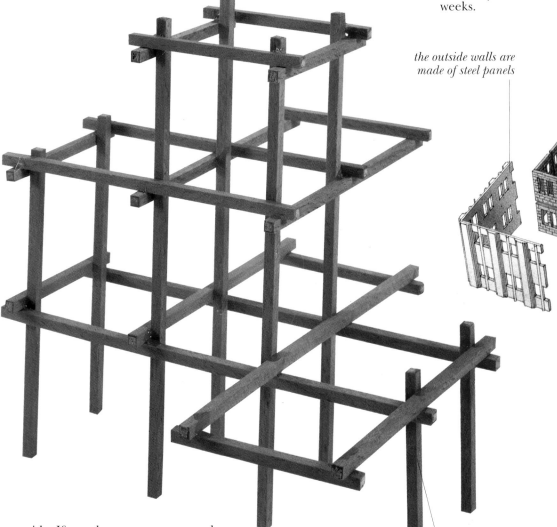

UNITY IS STRENGTH
What makes a frame very strong is the fact that, together, all its parts help to absorb forces coming from outside. If we take a group of just three matches joined together, the group is weak and unstable. However, if we link this group to lots of other groups, we get a much stronger structure. This is because the movement of an individual match is countered by the combined strength of the other matches.

the number of softwood joists joined together here, make this structure very strong

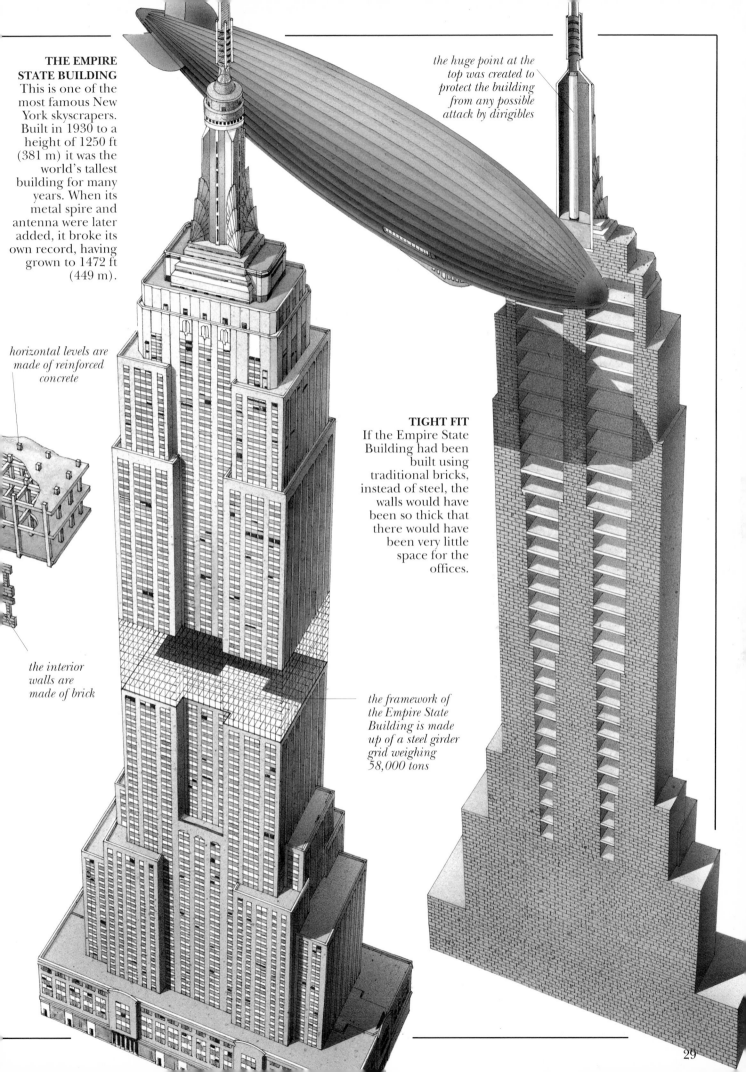

THE EMPIRE STATE BUILDING

This is one of the most famous New York skyscrapers. Built in 1930 to a height of 1250 ft (381 m) it was the world's tallest building for many years. When its metal spire and antenna were later added, it broke its own record, having grown to 1472 ft (449 m).

the huge point at the top was created to protect the building from any possible attack by dirigibles

horizontal levels are made of reinforced concrete

TIGHT FIT

If the Empire State Building had been built using traditional bricks, instead of steel, the walls would have been so thick that there would have been very little space for the offices.

the interior walls are made of brick

the framework of the Empire State Building is made up of a steel girder grid weighing 58,000 tons

THE ENEMIES OF BUILDINGS

Fire, wind and water have always been the enemies of buildings. In the past, when cities were built mostly in wood, fire was the major danger and ever a threat. In 1666 the Great Fire of London almost totally destroyed the city. But even today an electrical fault, among other things, is enough to cause fire to break out.

Wind, as it pushes against walls, is another danger to buildings. Usually the weight of a building is enough to resist strong winds. Skyscrapers can survive winds present at great heights if measures, such as those discussed below, have been taken to counter them.

Earthquakes are another threat, and are frequent in some places. There are two main safety measures which architects can take. Tall buildings are designed so that they bend rather than break. Smaller buildings are built using light structures: if they collapse in an earthquake, the falling buildings do not harm anybody.

THE TREE
The tree is a wonderful structure. Its roots, planted in the soil and spread out in a circle, are perfect foundations. They hold the tree in place when the wind makes the trunk bend.

RESISTING WIND
A skyscraper is designed to function like a tree, bending but not breaking in strong winds. Chicago's John Hancock Center narrows in height, so that there is less surface where the wind is stronger. The building is strengthened by triangular beams.

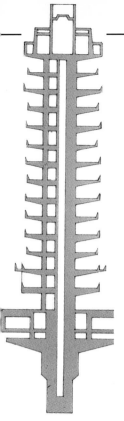

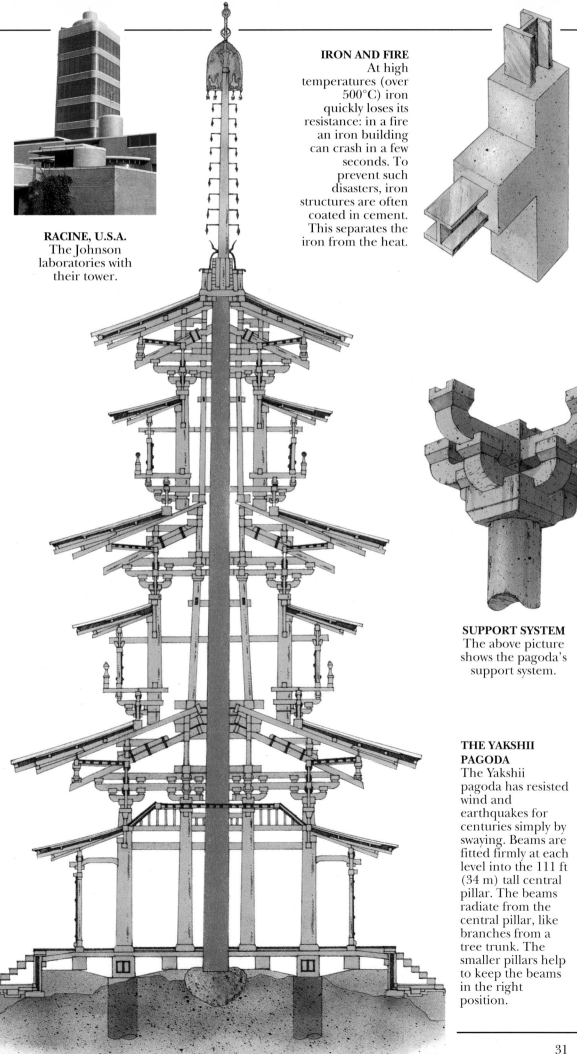

RACINE, U.S.A.
The Johnson laboratories with their tower.

IRON AND FIRE
At high temperatures (over 500°C) iron quickly loses its resistance: in a fire an iron building can crash in a few seconds. To prevent such disasters, iron structures are often coated in cement. This separates the iron from the heat.

BUILDINGS LIKE TREES
The Johnson building was designed by Frank Lloyd Wright in 1937-9. Its tower was added in 1950 and has a similar structure to that of a tree. The central column is like a trunk, on to which the various stories are attached.

RESISTANCE TO EARTHQUAKES
In Japan, where earthquakes are frequent, building damage has to be kept to the minimum. Traditional houses are low and have strong structures. Above all, though, buildings are light and flexible. Materials used are bamboo and wood, with walls often being made of paper.

SUPPORT SYSTEM
The above picture shows the pagoda's support system.

THE YAKSHII PAGODA
The Yakshii pagoda has resisted wind and earthquakes for centuries simply by swaying. Beams are fitted firmly at each level into the 111 ft (34 m) tall central pillar. The beams radiate from the central pillar, like branches from a tree trunk. The smaller pillars help to keep the beams in the right position.

SUSPENSION BRIDGES

The practice of designing bridges which hang has been followed for thousands of years. It is simpler and cheaper to stretch rope between two river banks than to build a massive bridge with stone and brick arches. But a rope bridge does not allow the passage of heavy loads, and only supports the weight of one or two people at the most.

This kind of structure did not change, though, until the arrival of steel. It then became possible to make hollow metal poles and supports so strong that even roads could be hung on them. Suspension bridges were given such a dramatic burst of new life, that bridges hundreds of feet in length suddenly seemed short. San Francisco's Golden Gate Bridge, built in 1937, was over three-quarters of a mile long.

THE GOLDEN GATE BRIDGE
The bridge over San Francisco Bay was built in 1937 by the architects Amman, Strauss, Moissief and Derleth.

LIANE BRIDGE
An explorer's drawing, showing a liane bridge in Africa at the end of the 19th century.

THE CLIFTON BRIDGE
Of the first suspension bridges, the Clifton Bridge (built 1829) at the mouth of the River Avon, near Bristol, England, is the most famous. It was designed by the engineer Isambard Brunel (1806-59).

COMPRESSION
In a reinforced concrete bridge the central arch and pillars can only resist compression stress, i.e., they work in compression.

the load of suspended stones acts as a counterfort

wooden planking

BAMBOO
In Tibet there are still bamboo suspension bridges – some over 230 ft (70 m) in length. Huts filled with stone at either end of the bridges act as counterforts.

braided bamboo

the trunks to which the canes are fixed are rotated and kept taut.

TRACTION
Only the counterforts of suspension bridges resist compression. The cables, however, resist traction stress, i.e., they work in traction.

CANTILEVER BRIDGES

The development of the railroad made it necessary to build new bridges over rivers and valleys. The cantilever bridge, invented in the second half of the 19th century, was a good answer to this need. Some idea of how it works can be seen by looking at the similar forces at play when a weightlifter prepares to lift weights over his or her head. The athlete's body, evenly balanced on slightly parted legs, is similar to the central pylon of the cantilever bridge. The arms are like the tie beams, and the barbell corresponds to the bridge level.

LIFTING WEIGHTS
As the weightlifter prepares to lift the weights, the forces are balanced in much the same way as they are in the cantilever bridge

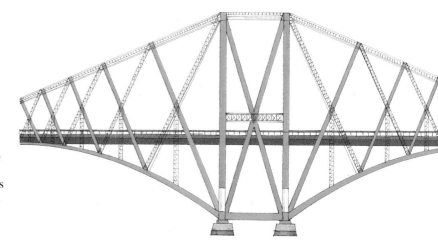

DRAWBRIDGE
This was the forerunner to the cantilever bridge. Two strong chains or beams support the solid wooden platform.

BAKER AND FOWLER'S EXPERIMENT
These two young boys are not especially strong. Yet because of their positions (similar to the positions of the pillars of a cantilever bridge), they can easily support the weight of the girl seated on the central plank. By setting up a similar experiment, the engineers Baker and Fowler convinced the public of their project's worth.

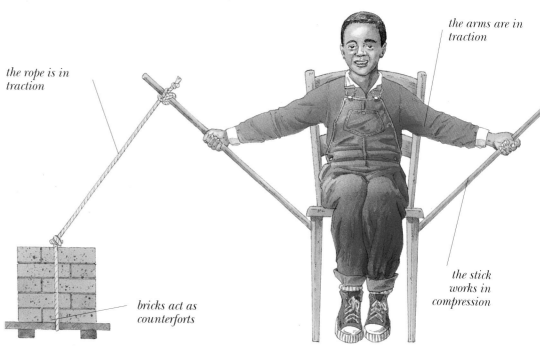

the rope is in traction

the arms are in traction

the stick works in compression

bricks act as counterforts

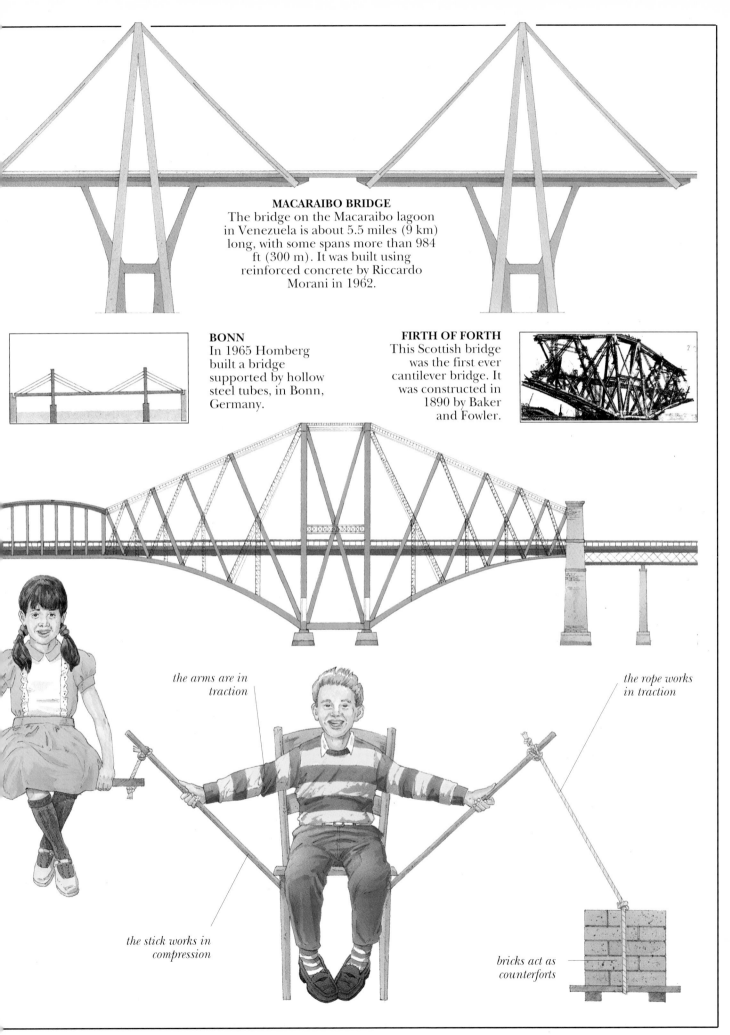

MACARAIBO BRIDGE
The bridge on the Macaraibo lagoon in Venezuela is about 5.5 miles (9 km) long, with some spans more than 984 ft (300 m). It was built using reinforced concrete by Riccardo Morani in 1962.

BONN
In 1965 Homberg built a bridge supported by hollow steel tubes, in Bonn, Germany.

FIRTH OF FORTH
This Scottish bridge was the first ever cantilever bridge. It was constructed in 1890 by Baker and Fowler.

the arms are in traction

the rope works in traction

the stick works in compression

bricks act as counterforts

CEMENT AND IRON: A GOOD COMBINATION

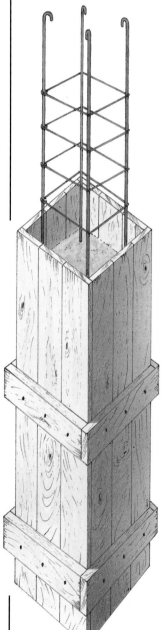

FRANÇOIS HENNEBIQUE
(1842 - 1921)
The French engineer who first successfully experimented with reinforced concrete.

In 1824 Joseph Aspdin, an Englishman, patented a more efficient cement than ones previously used. It was made of a mixture of lime and clay fired to a great heat. It was, at first, called artificial stone because of its appearance. Later, it was discovered that this cement had a surprising feature: in heat it expanded just like iron did. Experiments were then made on metal beams and pillars covered with cement. The combination was ideal, because the stone's ability to resist compression was united with iron's resistance to traction. Today, this material is known as reinforced concrete.

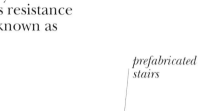

huge cranes lift the prefabricated parts into position

prefabricated stairs

REINFORCED CONCRETE
As well as its strength, reinforced concrete has another advantage: when the cement is made, it is liquid and sticky. It can be poured into molds and formed into different shapes. Since iron molds can be erected according to the size and shape needed, continuous structures can be made in just one casting, hardening in only a few weeks.

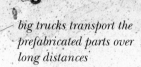

big trucks transport the prefabricated parts over long distances

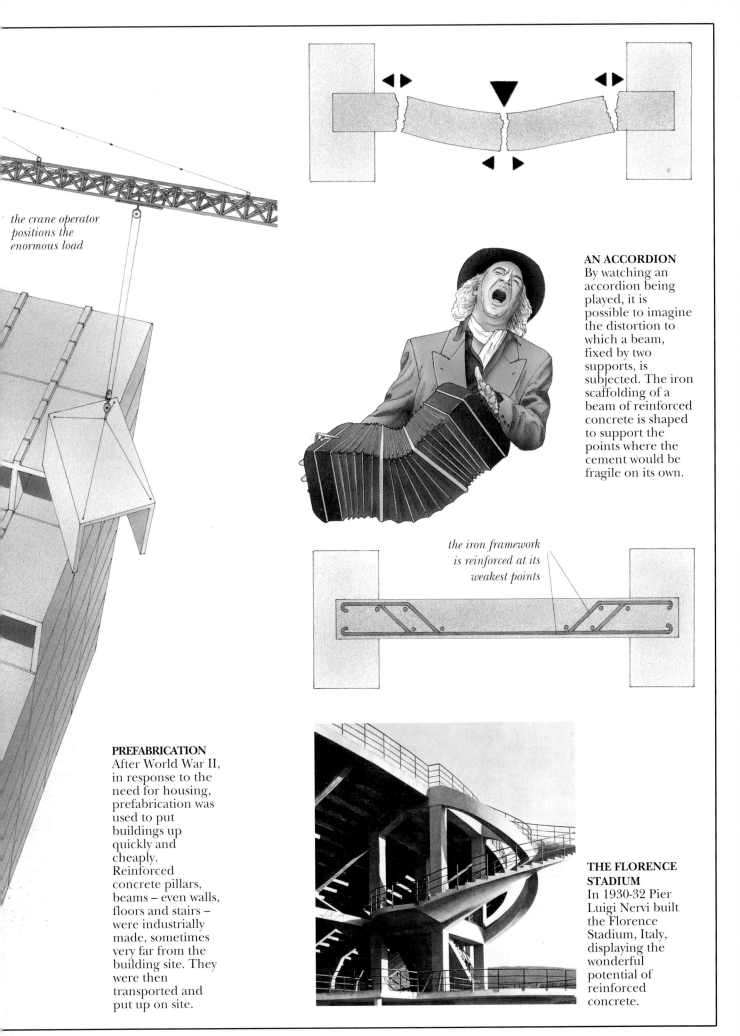

the crane operator positions the enormous load

AN ACCORDION
By watching an accordion being played, it is possible to imagine the distortion to which a beam, fixed by two supports, is subjected. The iron scaffolding of a beam of reinforced concrete is shaped to support the points where the cement would be fragile on its own.

the iron framework is reinforced at its weakest points

PREFABRICATION
After World War II, in response to the need for housing, prefabrication was used to put buildings up quickly and cheaply. Reinforced concrete pillars, beams – even walls, floors and stairs – were industrially made, sometimes very far from the building site. They were then transported and put up on site.

THE FLORENCE STADIUM
In 1930-32 Pier Luigi Nervi built the Florence Stadium, Italy, displaying the wonderful potential of reinforced concrete.

STRONG SHAPES

Materials become stronger or weaker according to the shapes they are given. Engineers and architects, working on the shape of materials, such as reinforced concrete, steel and even wood, have created strong but light structures.

Technology has taken many of its ideas from nature. Honeycomb, shells, spider webs, insect wings and the shape of certain leaves - all of these things have inspired a large number of both big and small inventions.

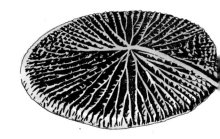

LEAF PATTERNS
Joseph Paxton, designer of the Crystal Palace in the 1851 Great Exhibition, London (see page 27), told admirers that the structure of the Palace was inspired by a leaf.

LIGHT BUT STRONG
A sheet of paper folded or simply curved becomes stronger than when flat.

FULL AND EMPTY
Take two metal cylinders of the same diameter, one solid and the other hollow: the first will be stronger. However, if we take a solid cylinder and a hollow tube, but with the hollow tube having a larger diameter than the cylinder, then the hollow tube will be the stronger.

EXPERIMENT
Find some paper, glue and scissors. Try making the same shapes as in the picture to the right. Experiment with other shapes. Can you find any which are as strong, or stronger, than the ones shown here.

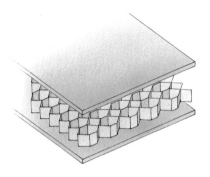

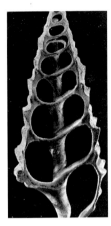

HONEYCOMB
Many doors are like a sandwich: two sheets of plywood are glued to cardboard formed like honeycomb.

CORRUGATED IRON
This is based on the idea of folding a sheet of paper into a fan. Rigid when standing, it can be rolled up for transport.

FRANCESCO BORROMINI
(1599 - 1665)
This Italian baroque architect designed one of his most original works, the dome of the Roman church of Sant'Ivo della Sapienza, by studying the sections of a shell.

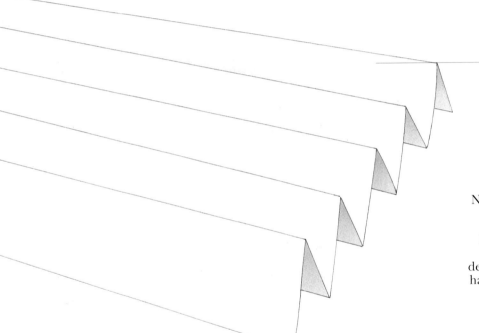

folding a sheet of paper into a fan shape, you get a strong and durable structure

PIER LUIGI NERVI
Nervi is one of the greatest engineers of reinforced concrete. In 1953, together with Marcel Breuer and Bernard Zehrfuss, he designed the UNESCO building in Paris. He designed the ceiling of the conference hall, pictured below, to have a fan-like appearance.

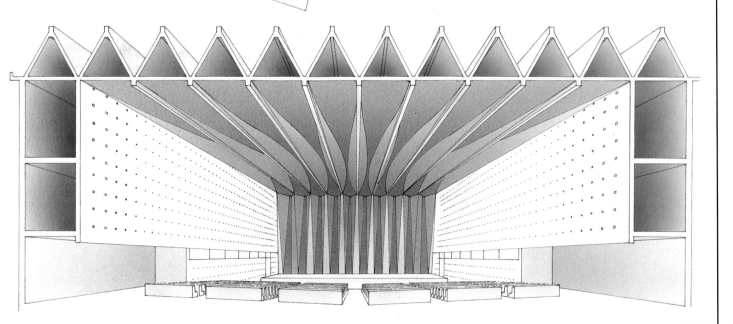

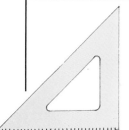

THE STRENGTH OF THE TRIANGLE

If we look around us closely, we can see that many familiar objects and architectural structures are triangular in design. Think of bicycle frames, certain chairs, bridges and trusses – they all have a triangular form. Why is this so? The reason is because, unlike the square frame, the triangular frame is rigid.

We can show this with simple experiments which compare two frames: one made with four sides and the other with three – as in the illustration at the bottom of this page. We can also test the triangle's strength in a fun way: by building a bridge of cards, as in the illustration shown on the right.

THE BICYCLE
A bicycle frame must be light and simple, but it must also be strong and rigid: the ideal frame was found to be made up of a grouping of triangles.

THE CHAIR
This light and collapsible canvas chair has a triangular structure.

LOOKING AT SOME DIFFERENT SHAPES
By nailing together four lengths of wood, a square, a rhombus or a parallelogram can be made. However, by nailing three lengths we can only make one shape – the triangle. Of the four shapes illustrated to the right, only the triangle is rigid. The triangle is, in fact, the only figure that cannot change its shape without a change in the length of its sides.

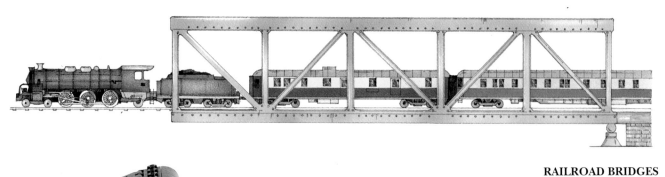

RAILROAD BRIDGES
Diagonal beams on railroad bridges give rigidity to a structure which is violently shaken by moving trains.

EXPERIMENT
Find some cards and some sticky tape. Try copying the above picture to make a model girder bridge. In spite of its lightness and apparent fragility, the bridge can easily support small loads.

PYRAMIDS
A pyramid shape, made up of four welded triangular frames, acted as the dome for the U.S. pavilion at the Expo, Montreal, in 1967.

LIGHT DOME
The architect Buckminster Fuller made light structures of many welded, or interlaying triangles.

Portable homes

Most buildings, ancient or modern, made in stone, brick or steel, are immobile. But there are many which have to be transportable. The nomads of the Sahara, for example, need to be able to take their homes with them. If a house is transportable, it has to be put up or taken down easily. Because of this, it has to be light, to have only a few parts, and to take up little space.

The tent of the nomads of the Sahara and Arabia is certainly the best answer. It is made of a fabric stretched with rope and placed on poles. The principle of the tent has inspired the design of many modern buildings.

REED MATTING
The mobile shelter of the nomadic shepherds of the Sudan is made of reeds.

PRACTICALITY
On special occasions such as a wedding, the Saharan nomads join all the various family tents together to form one huge tent.

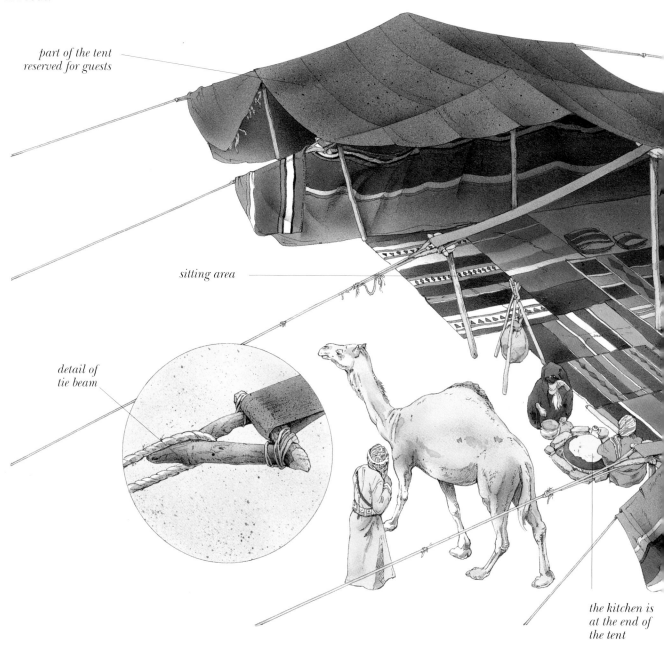

part of the tent reserved for guests

sitting area

detail of tie beam

the kitchen is at the end of the tent

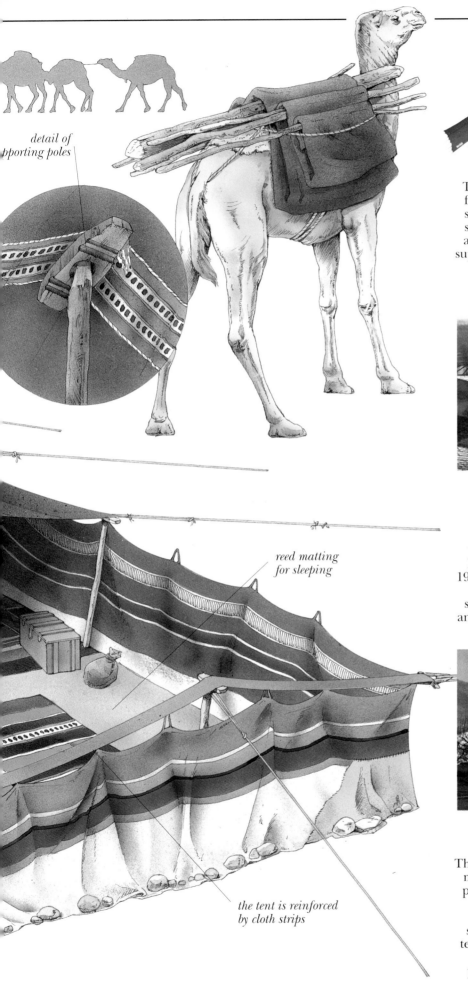

detail of supporting poles

reed matting for sleeping

the tent is reinforced by cloth strips

TENTS
The tents we use for camping are simple, efficient structures. Thin aluminum tubes support the canvas, which is stretched by ropes and pegs wedged in the earth. A tent provides a small shelter which weighs very little.

THE SPORTS VILLAGE, MUNICH
In the sports village, built in Munich for the 1972 Olympics, the buildings are spectacular steel and glass stretched structures. The village was designed by the German Otto Frei, who was the first person to experiment with structures such as these on a wide scale.

INFLATABLE STRUCTURES
The plastic roofs of many swimming pools and tennis courts are stretched structures. The tension is held by the inside air pressure being higher than the atmosphere outside. There is a tin chamber at the entrance, as in submarines, to stop the structure deflating when people enter or leave.

SOME LEADING FIGURES IN THE HISTORY OF BUILDINGS

In the past, scientists and technicians did not work well together. Scientists were dedicated to the "noble" arts of arithmetic, geometry, music and astronomy. They felt themselves superior to engineers, architects and artisans. This lack of cooperation slowed down the development of a sound structural theory: throughout the Roman, Medieval and even Renaissance period, the solution to structural problems was left to intuition and common sense. Problems were looked at as and when they occurred. If an especially good solution was found, this was added to the general store of knowledge.

Leonardo da Vinci was the first architect to see the limits of such a method and to try to find mathematical explanations to structural problems. Galileo Galilei was the first scientist to draw up a theoretical formula to some of these problems. The linking up between scientist and technician had begun.

From the 17th century on, the study of structure was firmly placed in the hands of mathematicians, and they developed its theory. Christopher Wren, famous for the building of London's St. Paul's Cathedral between 1675-1720, illustrates this change. He was a great mathematician, physicist and astronomer before he became interested in architecture.

VITRUVIO POLLIONE
(Ist century BC)
Roman architect from the time of Augustus. He wrote the only ancient architectural treatise known to us. A manuscript was discovered in a Swiss monastery in 1414. It contains valuable advice on building techniques, and it had great influence on Renaissance architects.

VILLARD DE HONNECOURT
(13th century)
French architect who left a design notebook illustrating the wide technical knowledge medieval builders owned. He also left lots of useful advice for solving different problems, from designing plans for a cathedral to making a machine.

The dome was an example of the leap from Gothic building methods to Renaissance style.

LEONARDO DA VINCI
(1452-1519)
Painter, sculptor, engineer, scientist and architect – the most representative figure of the Italian Renaissance. He was the first person to measure tension in an arch. His method of measuring the resistance of materials is still used today.

ANDREA PALLADIO
(1508-1580)
He was the architect who, more than anyone, helped spread Renaissance architecture beyond Italy. His treatise, the *Four Books of Architecture*, played an important role in this.

FILIPPO BRUNELLESCHI
(1337-1446)
The first and one of the major Renaissance architects. He formulated laws on perspective and designed the grand dome of Florence Cathedral.

GALILEO GALILEI
(1564-1642)
Physicist, mathematician and astronomer. He is considered the real

founder of modern scientific knowledge about the resistance of building materials.

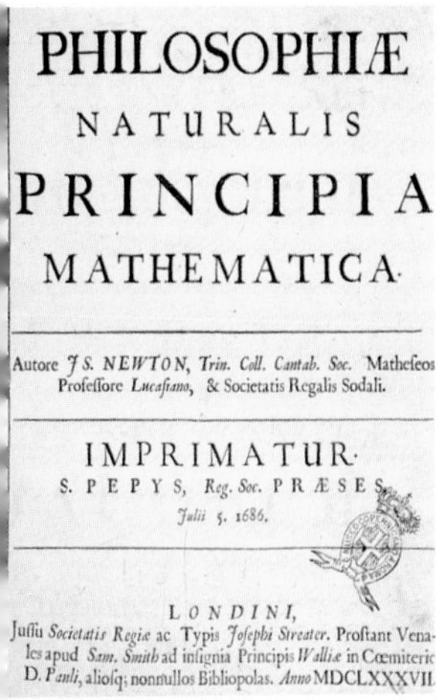
PHILOSOPHIÆ
NATURALIS
PRINCIPIA
MATHEMATICA.

Autore *J. S. NEWTON*, *Trin. Coll. Cantab. Soc.* Matheseos Professore *Lucasiano*, & Societatis Regalis Sodali.

IMPRIMATUR.
S. PEPYS, *Reg. Soc.* PRÆSES.
Julii 5. 1686.

LONDINI,
Jussu *Societatis Regiæ* ac Typis *Josephi Streater*. Prostant Venales apud *Sam. Smith* ad insignia Principis *Walliæ* in Cœmiterio D. *Pauli*, aliosq; nonnullos Bibliopolas. *Anno* MDCLXXXVII.

ISAAC NEWTON
(1642-1727)
He wrote the mathematical principles of natural philosophy in 1683, in which the law of universal attraction was put forward for the first time.

PHILIPPE DE LA HIRE
(1640-1718)
Mathematician and physicist. In 1695, he made the first serious attempt to form a theory on the arch. This theory was only appreciated a century later.

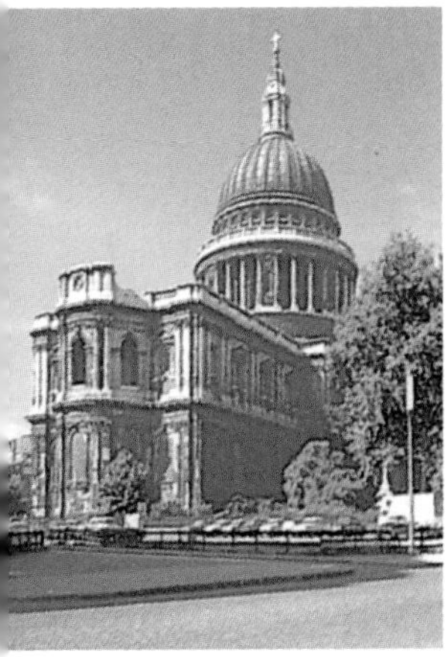

ROBERT HOOKE
(1635-1703)
CHRISTOPHER WREN
(1632-1723)
English friends who were brilliant scientists before becoming architects. Hooke was skilled in many areas, from astronomy to instrument design. He is famous for "Hooke's Law" on elasticity. Wren was an Oxford astronomy professor before becoming an architect at the age of 31. He built the dome of St. Paul's, the first ever dome in England.

LEONHARD EULER
(1707-1783)
The Swiss inventor of an important theory about the elasticity of materials.

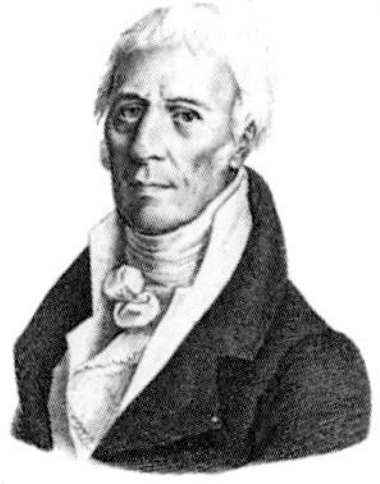

CHARLES-AUGUSTIN DE COULOMB
(1736-1806)
His theory on beams is still taught today in universities.

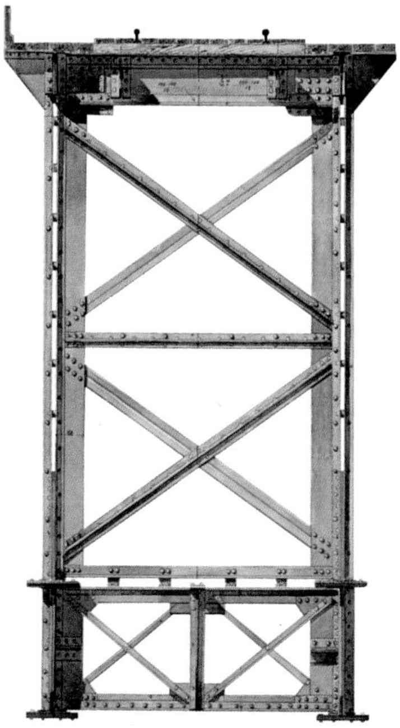

SCHOOL OF PONTS ET CHAUSSÉES
Founded in 1747 and led by Jean Rodolphe Perronet (1708-94), this was the first modern engineering school.

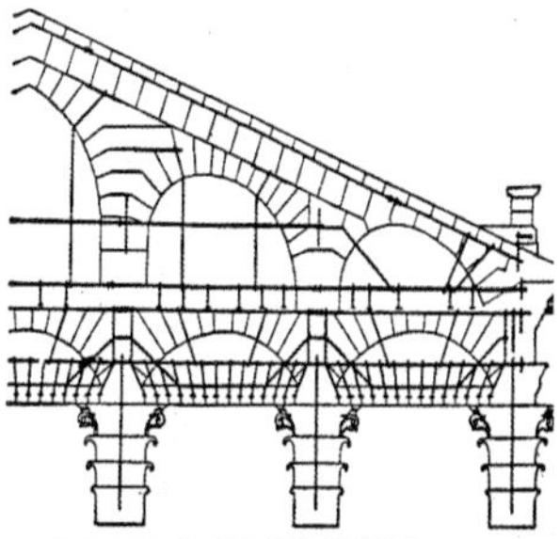

JACQUES GERMAIN SOUFFLOT
(1713-1780)
EMILAND MARIE GAUTHEY
(1732-1806)
They were the architect and engineer of St. Geneviève Church in Paris. They made stone and iron structures which worked along the same lines as reinforced concrete technology did later.

JOSEPH ASPDIN
(1779-1855)
He patented an artificial cement called Portland. He thought that his artificial stone was like Portland stone in color and hardness.

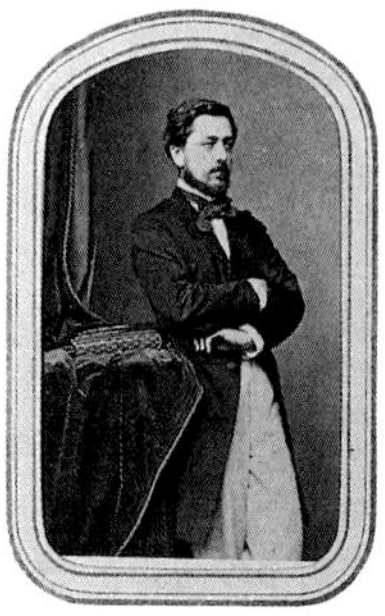

ALEXANDRE GUSTAVE EIFFEL
(1832-1923)
Engineer and entrepreneur. His famous Eiffel Tower established metal as a construction material. He designed the framework for the Statue of Liberty and many bridges, patenting a dismountable bridge system successfully used in many places.

FRANÇOIS HENNEBIQUE
(1842-1921)
The pioneer of reinforced concrete, which was used for the first time in 1879 and patented in 1894.

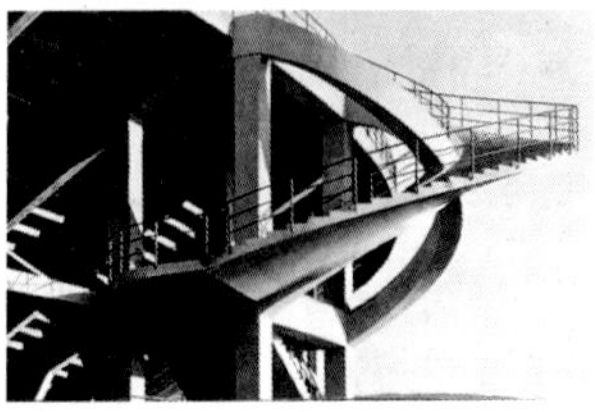

PIER LUIGI NERVI
(1891-1979)
Italian engineer and reinforced concrete specialist. He designed many projects, from Florence Stadium (1930) to the vast auditorium in the Vatican (1971).

JEAN PROUVÉ
(1901-1984)
French master of light metallic constructions. He had an important role in the invention of prefabricated buildings, such as houses or schools.

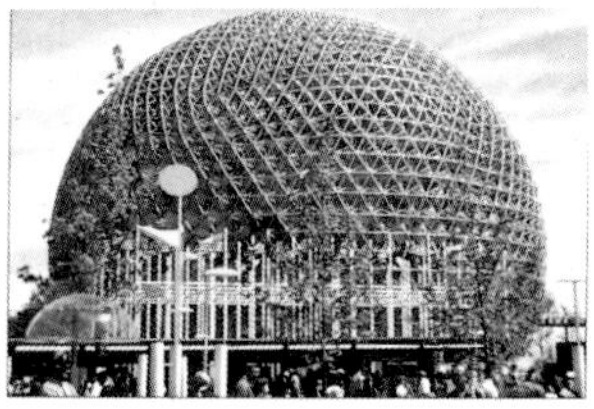

BUCKMINSTER FULLER
(1895-1983)
Inventor of the geodesic dome, a new structure using modern materials, such as light metal alloys and acrylic paneling.

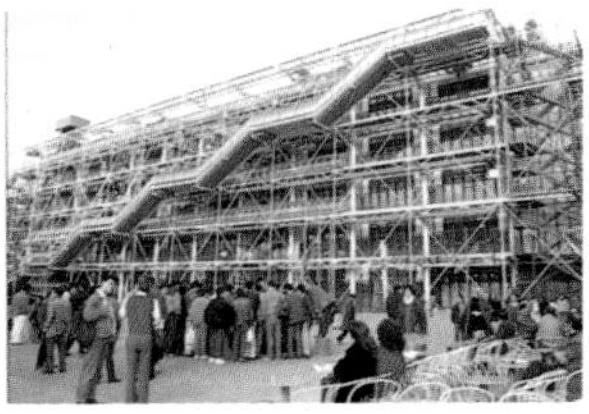

RENZO PIANO
(b. 1937)
RICHARD ROGERS
(b. 1933)
Designers of the Pompidou Center in Paris built between 1972-77. The building's structure is external, allowing large areas inside the building to be used to show works of art.

GLOSSARY

APSE Part of a church. It is usually semi circular in shape and covered by a semi dome.

ARCH Curved structure put over a door, window, bridge and so on. It often forms part of a wall.

ARCHITRAVE Horizontal stone or beam placed on the top of two walls or pillars. It forms the upper part of a trilith.

ASHLAR Stone block, more or less rectangular, often used for making arches and vaults. It can also be used as a covering material.

BARYCENTER The point at which the weight of an object is centered.

BEAM Horizontal part of a structure. It has to be made in a flexible material such as wood, steel or reinforced concrete.

BINDING Artificial material such as cement or glue, which can hold materials such as stone or brick firmly together.

CEMENT Grey powder, made from heating a mixture of limestone and clay. It is mixed with water and, as it sets, it becomes as hard as stone

CENTERING A support, usually made in wood. It holds up and gives shape to arches, vaults or domes while they are being built. Once the structures have been finished, the centerings are removed.

CLASSICAL ARCHITECTURE Ancient Greek and Roman architecture.

CLAY-BRICK Bricks, roofing tiles, hollow flat blocks etc made of fired clay.

COLUMN Vertical, usually circular post, used to support the weight of an overhanging structure, such as a ceiling or arch.

COMPRESSION The type of stress which tends to press down on a body or form.

CONCRETE Stone-like building material, made from a mixture of cement; sand and gravel. It is used for making beams and floors.

COUNTERFORT A pillar placed up against a wall. Due to its own weight, it absorbs the thrust of arches, roofs or vaults. It can be placed against a partition or linked to a building by one or more flying buttresses.

CUPOLA A rounded vault or dome forming the whole or part of a roof.

DOME A rounded vault, forming the roof of a building.

FLEXIBLE Pliant, not rigid. Wood is a flexible material, coping well with both compression and traction.

FLOOR Horizontal part of a building, made of such materials as wood, brick or tiles. It forms the base of a room on any of the stories of a building (e.g., ground floor, first floor, etc.).

FLYING BUTTRESS A connecting arch which passes on the thrust of the arches, roofs or vaults of a Gothic style building to a counterfort.

FOUNDATIONS Support bases for a building. They direct the weight of the building to the ground so as to give the buildings stability.

GALLERY Balcony or corridor which goes around a building, or part of it. It can be inside or outside a building.

KING POST The vertical pole placed in the center of a truss.

LIMESTONE Lime-based stone used as a building material. It can either be split or cut to make ashlars or ground down into a powder which is then used to make cement.

LOAD-BEARING Any of those vertical parts of a building which support a weight, for example, walls columns and pillars.

MASON A builder who works with stone or bricks.

MOLD A wooden or metal form into which concrete is poured. The mold is removed when the concrete has hardened and taken on the mold's shape.

NAVE The main part or body of a church.

PALLADIAN ARCHITECTURE The style influenced by the architect Palladio. Palladio is famous for his building known as "La Rotunda," in Vicenza, Italy.

PEDIMENT The triangular shape crowning the front of a classical style building.

PIER Any vertical feature with a load-bearing function.

PILLAR Vertical load-bearing structure such as a column.

PINNACLE Another word for spire.

PLINTH Support base for a pillar.

PLUMB LINE A line or cord with a weight attached to its end. It is used to find out whether a building is absolutely vertical.

PREFABRICATION Industrial process which consists of making some of the different parts of a building in specialized workshops. The parts are then assembled on the actual site.

REINFORCED CONCRETE Concrete strengthened by steel bars, strands, mesh, etc. placed inside before it hardens.

RENAISSANCE ARCHITECTURE The revival of the classical style of architecture which started in Italy and took place between the 14th and 16th centuries.

RIB A curved strip of stone, timber or metal, forming part of the framework of a dome.

RIGID Resistant, not bending. Stone is a rigid material and shatters easily.

ROOFING TILE Terracotta or similar material used for covering a roof to make it waterproof.

SCAFFOLDING Temporary structure made out of wood or steel. It is used to support workers and materials during building construction.

SPIRE Pyramid or cone-shaped feature, characteristic of the Gothic style. It forms the highest point of a building, or part of a building.

STABLE Secure, not subject to movement.

STATICS The area of physics in which the balance of solid objects, including the balance of buildings, is studied.

STRUT One of the two beams connecting the king post to the rafters of a truss.

SUBSIDENCE The gradual sinking of a building, or part of one, into the ground on which it stands.

SUSPENSIONS The horizontal parts of a building, such as floors or ceilings.

TAMBOUR Portion of a circular or many-sided room. It connects the dome to the pier.

THRUST The weight or pressing force of an object.

TIE BEAM A horizontal beam which holds the weight or thrust of a roof or arch.

TRACTION The type of stress which tends to lengthen or stretch a body or form.

TRANSEPT The part of a church lying at right angles to the nave.

TRILITH A structural system made of three parts: one horizontal (the architrave) and two vertical supports (the piers).

TRUSS Triangular structure supporting the roof. In its simplest form it is made of two angled beams, fixed at their ends to a horizontal beam. It can be made of wood, steel, iron or reinforced concrete.

TRUSS ROD Metal or wooden pole which absorbs the thrust of arches or vaults.

VAULT A number of arches radiating out from a central point. It is used to form a roof over a space in the inside of a building.

WARPING When wood changes shape as it dries, either shrinking or bowing.

INDEX

Page numbers in **bold** refer to illustrations.